TWENTY-FOUR
CHRISTMAS
CAROLS FOR
CLASSICAL
GUITAR

Published by
Wise Publications
14-15 Berners Street, London W1T 3LJ, UK.

Exclusive Distributors:
Music Sales Limited
Distribution Centre, Newmarket Road,
Bury St Edmunds, Suffolk IP33 3YB, UK.

Music Sales Pty Limited
20 Resolution Drive, Caringbah,
NSW 2229, Australia.

Order No. AM999119
ISBN 978-1-84938-328-8
This book © Copyright 2009 Wise Publications,
a division of Music Sales Limited.

Music arranged by Derek Jones.
Music processed by Paul Ewers Music Design.
Edited by Adrian Hopkins.

www.musicsales.com

Printed in the EU.

WISE PUBLICATIONS
part of The Music Sales Group
London/New York/Paris/Sydney/Copenhagen/Berlin/Tokyo/Madrid

AWAY IN A MANGER

Words: Traditional
Music by William Kirkpatrick
Classical guitar arrangement by Zachary Taylor

Away in a manger, no crib for a bed,
The little Lord Jesus laid down His sweet head;
The stars in the bright sky looked down where He lay,
The little Lord Jesus asleep in the hay.

The cattle are lowing, the baby awakes,
But little Lord Jesus no crying He makes.
I love Thee, Lord Jesus, look down from the sky,
And stay by my side until morning is nigh.

Be near me, Lord Jesus, I ask Thee to stay
Close by me forever, and love me, I pray!
Bless all the dear children in Thy tender care,
And fit us for heaven to live with Thee there.

Santa Clause Is Coming To Town

<Name>

Frosty The Snowman

<Name>

CHRISTIANS AWAKE

Words by John Byrom
Music by John Wainwright
Classical guitar arrangement by Zachary Taylor

Christians, awake, salute the happy morn,
Whereon the Saviour of the world was born;
Rise to adore the mystery of love,
Which hosts of Angels chanted from above;
With them the joyful tidings first begun
Of God Incarnate and the Virgin's Son.

THE COVENTRY CAROL

TRADITIONAL
CLASSICAL GUITAR ARRANGEMENT BY ZACHARY TAYLOR

Lullay, lullay, Thou little tiny Child,
By, by, lullay, lullay:
Lullay, Thou little tiny Child,
By, by, lullay, lullay?

Herod the king in his raging,
Charged he hath this day
His men of might, in his own sight,
All children young to slay.
Then woe is me, poor Child, for Thee,
And ever mourn and say,
For Thy parting nor say nor sing,
By, by, lullay, lullay.

CRADLED IN A MANGER, MEANLY

Words by George S. Rowe
Music by S. J. P. Dunman
Classical guitar arrangement by Zachary Taylor

Cradled in a manger, meanly
Laid the Son of Man His head;
Sleeping His first earthly slumber
Where the oxen had been fed.
Happy were those shepherds listening
To the holy angel's word;
Happy they within that stable,
Worshipping their infant Lord.

Happy all who hear the message
Of His coming from above;
Happier still who hail His coming,
And with praises greet His love.
Blessed Saviour, Christ most holy,
In a manger Thou didst rest;
Canst Thou stoop again, yet lower,
And abide within my breast?

DING DONG! MERRILY ON HIGH

Words by George Woodward
Music: traditional
Classical guitar arrangement by Zachary Taylor

Ding, dong, merrily on high
The Christmas bells are ringing;
Ding, dong, joyously reply
The angels all a-singing.
G-l-o-r-i-a, Hosanna in excelsis.

Ding, dong, carol all the bells,
Ring out the Christmas story;
Ding, dong, sound the good nowells,
God's Son has come in glory!
G-l-o-r-i-a, Hosanna in excelsis.

THE FIRST NOWELL

TRADITIONAL
CLASSICAL GUITAR ARRANGEMENT BY ZACHARY TAYLOR

The first Nowell the Angel did say,
Was to certain poor shepherds in fields as they lay;
In fields where they lay keeping their sheep,
On a cold winter's night that was so deep.
Nowell, Nowell, Nowell, Nowell,
Born is the King of Israel.

FOR UNTO US A CHILD IS BORN
(FROM 'MESSIAH')

Words compiled from Holy Scripture by Charles Jennens
Music by George Frideric Handel
Classical guitar arrangement by Zachary Taylor

Unto us a child is born!
King of all creation,
Came He to a world forlorn,
The Lord of ev'ry nation.

Cradled in a stall was He
With sleepy cows and asses;
But the very beasts could see
That He all men surpasses.

GOD REST YOU MERRY, GENTLEMEN

Traditional
Classical guitar arrangement by Zachary Taylor

God rest you merry, gentlemen,
Let nothing you dismay,
Remember Christ our Saviour
Was born on Christmas Day,
To save us all from Satan's pow'r
When we were gone astray;
O tidings of comfort and joy,
Comfort and joy,
O tidings of comfort and joy.

GOOD CHRISTIAN MEN REJOICE

Words by J.M. Neale
Music: Traditional
Classical guitar arrangement by Zachary Taylor

Good Christian men, rejoice
With heart, and soul, and voice;
Give ye heed to what we say:
News! News!
Jesus Christ is born today:
Ox and ass before Him bow,
And He is in the manger now.
Christ is born today!

GOOD KING WENCESLAS

WORDS BY J.M. NEALE
MUSIC: TRADITIONAL
CLASSICAL GUITAR ARRANGEMENT BY ZACHARY TAYLOR

Good King Wenceslas look'd out
On the Feast of Stephen,
When the snow lay round about,
Deep, and crisp, and even:
Brightly shone the moon that night,
Though the frost was cruel,
When a poor man came in sight,
Gathering winter fuel.

"Hither, page, and stand by by me,
If thou know'st it, telling,
Yonder peasant, who is he?
Where and what his dwelling?"
"Sire, he lives a good league hence,
Underneath the mountain;
Right against the forest fence,
By Saint Agnes' fountain."

HARK! THE HERALD ANGELS SING

Words by Charles Wesley
Music by Felix Mendelssohn
Classical guitar arrangement by Zachary Taylor

Hark! The herald-angels sing
Glory to the new-born King,
Peace on earth, and mercy mild,
God and sinners reconciled.
Joyful, all ye nations rise,
Join the triumph of the skies;
With the Angelic host proclaim;
"Christ is born in Bethlehem."
Hark! The herald-angels sing
Glory to the new-born King.

HERE WE COME A-WASSAILING

TRADITIONAL
CLASSICAL GUITAR ARRANGEMENT BY ZACHARY TAYLOR

Here we come a-wassailing
Among the leaves so green,
Here we come a-wandering,
So fair to be seen.

Love and joy come to you,
And to you your wassail too,
And God bless you and send you
A happy New Year,
And God send you a happy New Year.

Our wassail-cup is made,
Of the rosemary tree,
And so is your beer
Of the best barley.

Love and joy come to you,
And to you your wassail too,
And God bless you and send you
A happy New Year,
And God send you a happy New Year.

We are not daily beggars
That beg from door to door,
But we are neighbour's children
Whom you have seen before.

Love and joy come to you,
And to you your wassail too,
And God bless you and send you
A happy New Year,
And God send you a happy New Year.

THE HOLLY AND THE IVY

TRADITIONAL
CLASSICAL GUITAR ARRANGEMENT BY ZACHARY TAYLOR

The rising of the sun,
And the running of the deer,
The playing of the merry organ,
Sweet singing in the choir.

The holly bears a berry,
As red as any blood;
And Mary bore sweet Jesus Christ,
For to do us sinners good.

The rising of the sun,
And the running of the deer,
The playing of the merry organ,
Sweet singing in the choir.

The holly and the ivy,
When they are both full grown,
Of all the trees that live in the wood,
The holly bears the crown.

The rising of the sun,
And the running of the deer,
The playing of the merry organ,
Sweet singing in the choir.

The holly bears a blossom,
As white as the lily flower;
And Mary bore sweet Jesus Christ,
To be our sweet Saviour.

IN THE BLEAK MIDWINTER

WORDS BY CHRISTINA ROSSETTI
MUSIC BY GUSTAV HOLST
CLASSICAL GUITAR ARRANGEMENT BY ZACHARY TAYLOR

In the bleak mid-winter,
Frosty wind made moan,
Earth stood hard as iron,
Water like a stone;
Snow had fallen, snow on snow,
Snow on snow,
In the bleak mid-winter,
Long ago.

Our God, Heaven cannot hold Him,
Nor earth sustain;
Heaven and earth shall flee away
When He comes to reign:
In the bleak mid-winter
A stable-place sufficed
The Lord God Almighty,
Jesus Christ.

IT CAME UPON A MIDNIGHT CLEAR

WORDS BY EDMUND HAMILTON SEARS
MUSIC BY RICHARD STORRS WILLIS
CLASSICAL GUITAR ARRANGEMENT BY ZACHARY TAYLOR

It came upon the midnight clear,
That glorious song of old,
From Angels bending near the earth
To touch their harps of gold;
"Peace on the earth, good-will to men,
From Heaven's all-gracious King":
The world in solemn stillness lay
To hear the Angels sing.

JINGLE BELLS

Words & Music by J.S. Pierpont
Classical guitar arrangement by Zachary Taylor

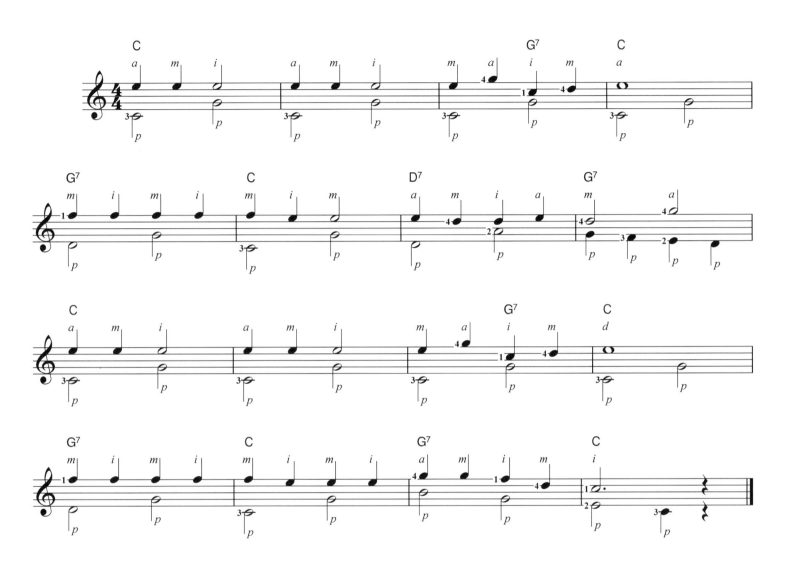

Jingle bells! Jingle bells!
Jingle all the way!
Oh, what fun it is to ride
In a one-horse open sleigh!
Oh, Jingle bells! Jingle bells!
Jingle all the way!
Oh, what fun it is to ride
In a one-horse open sleigh!

LITTLE JESUS (ROCKING CAROL)

Traditional
Classical guitar arrangement by Zachary Taylor

Little Jesus, sweetly sleep,

Do not stir,

We will lend a coat of fur.

We will rock you, rock you, rock you,

We will rock you, rock you, rock you,

See the fur to keep you warm,

Snuggly round your tiny form.

O COME ALL YE FAITHFUL

WORDS & MUSIC BY JOHN FRANCIS WADE
Classical guitar arrangement by Zachary Taylor

O come, all ye faithful,
Joyful and triumphant,
O come ye, O come ye to Bethlehem;
Come and behold Him,
Born the King of Angels;

O come, let us adore Him,
O come, let us adore Him,
O come, let us adore Him,
Christ, the Lord.

God of God,
Light of Light,
Lo, He abhors not the Virgin's womb,
Very God,
Begotten, not created:

O come, let us adore Him,
O come, let us adore Him,
O come, let us adore Him,
Christ, the Lord.

O LITTLE TOWN OF BETHLEHEM

WORDS BY PHILLIPS BROOKS
MUSIC BY LEWIS REDNER
CLASSICAL GUITAR ARRANGEMENT BY ZACHARY TAYLOR

O little town of Bethlehem,
How still we see thee lie!
Above thy deep and dreamless sleep
The silent stars go by,
Yet in the dark street shineth,
The everlasting Light;
The hopes and fears of all the years
Are met in thee tonight.

O morning stars, together
Proclaim the holy birth,
And praises sing to God the King,
And peace to men on earth;
For Christ is born of Mary;
And, gathered all above,
While mortals sleep, the angels keep
Their watch of wandering love.

ONCE IN ROYAL DAVID'S CITY

Words by Cecil Alexander
Music by Henry Gauntlett
Classical guitar arrangement by Zachary Taylor

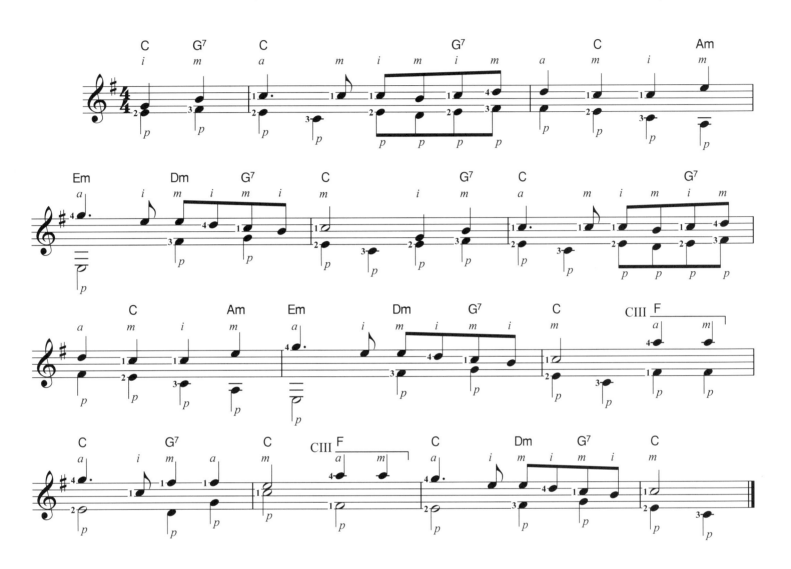

Once in Royal David's city,
Stood a lowly cattle shed,
Where a mother laid her Baby
In a manger for His bed;
Mary was that Mother mild,
Jesus Christ her little Child.

He came down to earth from Heaven
Who is God and Lord of all,
And His shelter was a stable,
And His cradle was a stall;
With the poor, the mean, and lowly,
Lived on earth our Saviour Holy.

SILENT NIGHT

Words by Joseph Mohr
Music by Franz Gruber
Classical guitar arrangement by Zachary Taylor

Silent night! Holy night;

All is calm, all is bright;

Round yon Virgin Mother and Child!

Holy Infant so tender and mild,

Sleep in heavenly peace,

Sleep in heavenly peace.

WHILE SHEPHERDS WATCHED

Words by Nahum Tate
Music: Traditional
Classical guitar arrangement by Zachary Taylor

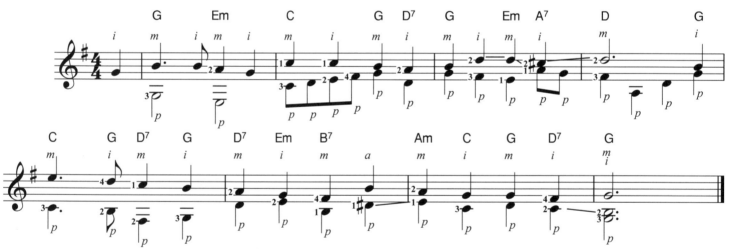

"To you in David's town this day
Is born of David's line
A saviour, Who is Christ the Lord;
And this shall be the sign:

"The heavenly Babe you there shall find
To human view display'd
All meanly wrapp'd in swathing bands,
And in a manger laid."

While shepherds watch'd their flocks by night,
All seated on the ground,
The Angel of the Lord came down,
And glory shone around.

"Fear not," said he; for might dread
Had seized their troubled mind;
"Glad tidings of great joy I bring
To you and all mankind.

WE THREE KINGS OF ORIENT ARE

Words & Music by John Henry Hopkins
Classical guitar arrangement by Zachary Taylor

We three kings of Orient are;
Bearing gifts we traverse afar
Field and fountain, moor and mountain,
Following yonder star.

O Star of wonder, star of night,
Star with royal beauty bright,
Westward leading, still proceeding,
Guide us to Thy perfect light.

WE WISH YOU A MERRY CHRISTMAS

Traditional
Classical guitar arrangement by Zachary Taylor

We wish you a Merry Christmas,
We wish you a Merry Christmas;
We wish you a Merry Christmas,
And a happy New Year!

Good tidings we bring,
To you and your kin,
We wish you a Merry Christmas,
And a happy New Year.

Oh, bring us some figgy pudding,
Oh, bring us some figgy pudding,
Oh, bring us some figgy pudding,
And bring it out here!

Good tidings we bring,
To you and your kin,
We wish you a Merry Christmas,
And a happy New Year.

We won't go until we've got some,
We won't go until we've got some,
We won't go until we've got some,
So bring some out here.

Good tidings we bring,
To you and your kin,
We wish you a Merry Christmas,
And a happy New Year.

1 2 3 4 5 6 7 8 9